Big Cats,  Little Cats

A Visual Guide to the World's Cats

FIREFLY BOOKS

Jim Medway

Contents

North American Cats

Cat breeds from the United States and Canada, including the lovable Maine Coon, the stripy Toyger, and the hairless Sphynx.

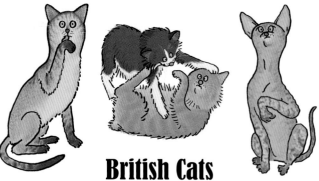

British Cats

Cats that come from places in Britain, such as the short-tailed Manx from the Isle of Man, and the curly-haired Devon Rex from Devon.

European Cats

Cat breeds from Europe, such as the ancient Norwegian Forest Cat, and the Toybob, the world's smallest domestic cat, from Russia.

Asian Cats

Many of the world's most popular breeds come from Asia, including the elegant Siamese, the affectionate Burmese, and the regal Persian.

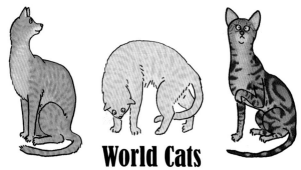

World Cats

Here are some of the rarer cat breeds from around the world, including the Australian Mist, the Egyptian Mau, and the Somali.

Big Cats

The great wild cats of the world, including the Lion, Tiger, Cheetah, Leopard, and Jaguar. Many of these species are now endangered. 20

Kittens

Follow the dotted lines to help find the kittens of adorable cats featured in the book. 16

Cubs

Follow the dotted lines to help find the cubs of big-cat species from around the world. 22

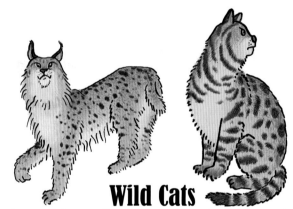

Wild Cats

The world's small wild cats from South America, North America, Europe, Asia, and Africa. 24

Cats Index

Interesting facts about all the cats – big, small, domestic and wild – featured in the book. 28

North American Cats

Maine Coon

Shorthaired Colorpoint

Cheetoh

Highlander

Ojos Azules

Smooth and Longhaired American Curl

Javanese

Exotic Shorthair

Foldex Cat

Lykoi

Minskin

American
Wirehair

Chantilly-
Tiffany

LaPerm

Savannah

American
Bobtail

California
Spangled

Munchkin

North American Cats (continued)

Bambino

Minuet

York Chocolate

Nebelung

American Shorthair

Oriental Shorthair

Serengeti

Sphynx

Ragdoll

Selkirk Rex

Snowshoe

Toyger

Pixie-bob

Ragamuffin

Tonkinese

Ocicat

Oriental
Bicolor

British Cats

British
Shorthair

Scottish
Fold

Manx

Asian

Asian Semi-
longhair

Coupari

Havana Brown

British Longhair

Cymric

Cornish Rex

Burmilla

Devon Rex

European Cats

Aegean

Toybob

Russian Blue

Russian Tabby

German Rex

Russian Black

Russian White

Donskoy

Kurilian Bobtail

Norwegian Forest Cat

European
Burmese

Serrade
Petit

European
Shorthair

Chartreux

Perfold

Ukrainian
Levkoy

Cyprus

Siberian

Peterbald

Asian Cats

Burmese

Thai

Singapura

Bengal

Bombay

Turkish
Angora

Dragon Li

Birman

Korat

Mekong
Bobtail

Siamese

Raas

Suphalak

Japanese
Bobtail

Balinese

Persian
(modern)

Asian Cats (continued)

Thai Lilac

Persian
(traditional)

Khao Manee

Sam Sawet

Korn Ja

Himalayan

Turkish Van

World Cats

Brazilian
Shorthair

Sokoke

Somali

Abyssinian

Arabian Mau

Chausie

Australian
Mist

Egyptian
Mau

Kittens

Exotic
Shorthair

Dragon Li

Maine Coon

Persian
(traditional)

American
Shorthair

Norwegian
Forest Cat

Himalayan

Russian
Blue

British
Shorthair

Siamese

Scottish
Fold

Bengal

Abyssinian

Nebelung

Siberian

Ragdoll

Pixie-bob

Burmese

Munchkin

Ragamuffin

Sphynx

Cornish Rex

Big Cats

Cougar

Jaguar

Snow
Leopard

African Lion

Asiatic
Cheetah

Sunda
Clouded
Leopard

Tiger

Clouded
Leopard

African
Cheetah

Amur
Leopard

Asiatic Lion

Cubs

Asiatic Lion

Tiger

Amur
Leopard

African
Cheetah

Asiatic
Cheetah

Snow
Leopard

African Lion

Jaguar

Sunda
Clouded
Leopard

Clouded
Leopard

Cougar

Wild Cats

Oncilla

Canadian
Lynx

Caracal

Rusty-
spotted Cat

Pampas Cat

Black-footed
Cat

Sand Cat

Margay

Bornean Bay
Cat

Eurasian
Lynx

Iberian Lynx

Iriomote Cat

Andean
Mountain
Cat

Jungle Cat

African
Golden Cat

Wild Cats (continued)

Kodkod

Marbled Cat

European
Wild Cat

Fishing Cat

Serval

Leopard Cat

Asian
Golden Cat

Geoffroys'
Cat

Ocelot

Bobcat

Chinese
Mountain Cat

Flat-headed
Cat

Pallas's Cat

Jaguarundi

27

Cats Index

Abyssinian
First shown at Crystal Palace in London, England in 1871, the Abyssinian is thought to come from Abyssinia (Ethiopia) in North Africa. 15, 18

Aegean
These cats come from the Cycladic Islands near Greece. They like water and fishing. 10

African Cheetah
The world's fastest land animal, the Cheetah can reach speeds of 70 miles an hour. 21, 22

African Golden Cat
The least-studied of all wild cats, the African Golden Cat is very rare. It eats mainly rodents. 25

African Lion
Lions live together in groups known as prides." They normally live for about 12 years. 20, 23

American Bobtail
This very affectionate breed has a short tail that it can wag when it is happy. 5

American Curl
Adult American Curls have curled ears. Kittens are born with straight ears, which start to change at around three months. 4

American Shorthair
America's early settlers from Europe brought cats with them aboard their ships to catch mice and rats. The American Shorthair is descended from these cats. 6, 16

American Wirehair
These cats have wiry, springy coats, and otherwise are much like American Shorthairs. 5

Amur Leopard
These endangered cats live in China and Russia. There may be fewer than 100 of them left in the wild. 21, 22

Andean Mountain Cat
This small cat from South America is about the same size as a domestic cat, but its thick fur and bushy tail make it look bigger. 25

Arabian Mau
This breed is believed to be over a thousand years old. It originally came from the deserts of Arabia. 15

Asian
Also known as the "Malayan," this breed is very similar to the Burmese, from which it was originally bred. 8

Asian Golden Cat
Asian Golden Cats are also known as "Fire Cats" in Thailand and Burma, and "Rock Cats" in China. 26

Asian Semi-longhair
A gentle cat, this breed is also called "Tiffany." It is known to mew and cry a good deal, especially at night. 8

Asiatic Cheetah
These rare wild cats can now be found only in Iran. Once they roamed over India, Pakistan, Russia, Iran, and the Middle East. 20, 22

Asiatic Lion
Also known as the "Indian Lion," this cat is smaller than the African Lion. There are only a few hundred Asiatic Lions left in the wild. 21, 22

Australian Mist
Developed in Australia, this breed is a cross between a Burmese, an Abyssinian, and other shorthaired cats. 15

Balinese
A longhaired version of the Siamese, the Balinese comes in the Siamese point colors of seal, chocolate, blue, and lilac; and has sapphire-blue eyes and a silky coat. 13

Bambino
"Bambino" means "baby" in Italian, and this breed was created to look like a kitten. It is hairless, and has short legs. 6

Bengal
The Bengal was created by breeding house cats with the wild Asian Leopard Cat. 12, 18

Birman
Believed to be descended from temple cats of ancient Burma, the Birman has pure-white paws called "socks." 12

Black-footed Cat
This is the smallest wild cat in South Africa. It will sometimes hide its prey to return later and eat it. 24

Bobcat
Found in North America, the Bobcat looks similar to other Lynx cats. It is twice the size of a domestic cat. 27

Bombay
This sturdy breed has a sleek, almost panther-like black coat, and bright-yellow eyes. 12

Bornean Bay Cat
An endangered species, the Bornean Bay Cat has stripes running down its small head. 25

Brazilian Shorthair
This cat is believed to be descended from cats brought to Brazil by the Portuguese in around 1500. 15

British Longhair
The breed is identical to the British Shorthair, apart from the length of its coat. 9

British Shorthair
This is one of the oldest cat breeds. It has a chunky body, thick coat, and broad face. The Cheshire Cat, a character in Lewis Carroll's 1865 novel *Alice's Adventures in Wonderland*, was based on a British Shorthair. 8, 17

Burmese
Most Burmese have green eyes, but some have yellow or blue eyes. 12, 19

Burmilla
With distinctive dark outlines to the nose, lips and eyes, the Burmilla has a sweet face. It has a silver-gray coat and its large round eyes are often green. 9

California Spangled
Bred to look like a wild cat, this cat is a mixture of an Abyssinian, American Shorthair, and a British Shorthair. It has spots like those of the Ocelot or Leopard Cat. 5

Canadian Lynx
Slightly larger than Bobcats, these wild cats live in Canada and Alaska. They eat mainly hares. 24

Caracal
These wild cats have large black tufts on their ears, black stripes on their faces, and light patches around the eyes and mouth. 24

Chantilly-Tiffany
This semi-longhaired cat has a soft and silky coat. 5

Chartreux
Sometimes called the national cat of France, the Chartreux is always blue in color and has orange eyes. It is a very old breed dating from the Middle Ages. 11

Chausie
The Chausie has a long face and looks like a Cougar. It was bred from a Jungle Cat and a domestic cat. 15

Cheetoh
A mixture of the Bengal and the Ocicat, the Cheetoh is one of the newer breeds. Unusually, its hind legs are slightly longer than its front legs. 4

Chinese Mountain Cat
Also known as the "Chinese Desert Cat," this wild cat has sandy-colored fur and a black-tipped tail. 27

Clouded Leopard
These wild cats live in Asia. They have very long tails, which help with their balance when they climb trees. 21, 23

Cornish Rex
These cats are also known as "Greyhound" cats because of their muscular bodies and their running style. They have large ears and very fine, soft, wavy coats, which come in many colors. 9, 19

Cougar
Also known as the "Mountain Lion" or "Panther," the Cougar is the second-largest cat in North America. It cannot roar, but purrs like a house cat. 20, 23

Burmese

Coupari
A longhaired version of the Scottish Fold, the Coupari also has little folded ears. 8

Cymric
This breed is a longhaired Manx. Both the Cymric and the Manx come from the Isle of Man, an island in the Irish Sea between Britain and Ireland. 9

Cyprus
According to legend, St. Helen brought cats from Egypt to Cyprus in the fourth century to rid the island of snakes and vermin. This breed is believed to be descended from those cats. 11

Devon Rex
This rare breed has been called the "pixie" of the cat world because of its large eyes and ears, its short muzzle, and its thick, curly coat. 9

Donskoy
A rare breed from Russia, the Donskoy has hairless skin and wrinkles all over its body. It has elongated webbed fingers. 10

Dragon Li
Also called the "Chinese Li Hua," this rare cat has a golden brown mackerel tabby pattern to its coat. 12, 16

Cyprus

Egyptian Mau
One of the oldest domestic breeds, this is one of the very few that has naturally-occurring spots on its coat. It has green eyes. 15

Eurasian Lynx
With strong legs and web-like feet that help them to walk on snow, most Eurasian Lynx live in Russia. 25

Egyptian Mau

European Burmese
The loyal and affectionate European Burmese is particularly good with children. 11

European Shorthair
Also called the "Celtic Shorthair," this very old breed comes from Northern Europe. 11

European Wild Cat
Although they look very similar to domestic cats, these wild cats cannot be kept as pets. They live in Scotland, Spain, and other parts of Europe. 26

Exotic Shorthair
Calm and affectionate, the Exotic Shorthair has a flat nose and face, and dense fur. 4, 16

Fishing Cat
These wild cats come from Southeast Asia, where they live near rivers, swamps, and lakes. They eat mainly fish. 26

Flat-headed Cat
A very rare small cat from Southeast Asia, the Flat-headed Cat has wide eyes and a flat skull, and is very good at catching fish. 27

Foldex Cat
A mix of the Scottish Fold and the Exotic Shorthair, the Foldex Cat has little ears that fold over its face, and round eyes. It comes from Canada. 5

Geoffroys' Cat
Found in South America, this is one of the smallest of the wild cats. About the size of a domestic cat, it has black spots, and pale fur on its underbelly. 27

German Rex
This German breed has long, thin legs and thick, curly hair. 10

Havana Brown
This chocolate-brown cat has a short coat that needs very little grooming. It has mesmerizing green eyes. 9

Highlander
The Highlander is a mix of the Desert Lynx and the Jungle Curl. It has a short bobtail and curled ears. 4

Himalayan
Created by crossing a Persian with a Siamese, this cat has a long colorpoint coat and blue eyes. 14, 17

Iberian Lynx
Found only in southern Spain, this lynx feeds mainly on rabbits. 25

Eurasian Lynx

Iriomote Cat
This is a very rare small cat related to the Leopard Cat. It comes from the remote islands of Iriomote in northern Japan. 25

Jaguar
The Jaguar lives in South America and is the third-largest cat after the Tiger and the Lion. Its name means "he who kills in one leap." 20, 23

Jaguarundi
The Jaguarundi is a wild cat from Central and South America. It is active during the day and hunts on the ground rather than in trees. 27

Japanese Bobtail
From Japan, this cat has a "bobtail," like a rabbit's tail. 13

Javanese
Similar to the Shorthaired Colorpoint, the Javanese is not from Java or Indonesia, but was first bred in America. 4

Jungle Cat
When they are born, Jungle Cats have spots, but these gradually fade away. The cats "talk" a lot and, unlike most wild breeds, they hunt during the day. 25

Khao Manee
A rare breed from Thailand, this is the most expensive cat in the world. Those with different-colored eyes are the rarest. 14

Kodkod
Kodkods are the smallest wild cats of South America, and live in Chile and central Argentina. They are excellent climbers. 26

Korat
Korats came from Thailand. They are considered to be lucky cats. 13

Korn Ja
Originally from Thailand, this cat is believed to bring good luck. Its coat is all black and it has yellow eyes. 14

Kurilian Bobtail
A very popular cat in Russia, the Kurilian Bobtail is a strong cat known to like fishing and hunting. It originally comes from the Kurilian Islands that lie between Russia and Japan. 10

LaPerm
This American breed is named for its "curly" hair. It is a Rex breed, so has soft, short fur. LaPerms are not related to any other Rex breeds. 5

Leopard Cat
In captivity, this wild cat can live up to 15 years. It is the most common wild cat in Southeast Asia. 26

Lykoi
The word "lykoi" means "wolf" in Greek. The cat is also known as the "Werewolf" cat, because its

Cats Index

face has a werewolfish appearance. The Lykoi is partially or almost entirely hairless. 5

Maine Coon
A highly popular cat, the Maine Coon is one of the oldest breeds in America. A big cat with tufted ears, it loves water and has a thick, waterproof coat. 4, 16

Manx
The Manx, like the Cymric, does not have a tail. It has very strong back legs and is one of the best jumpers in the cat world. 8

Marbled Cat
Related to the Asian Golden Cat and the Bornean Bay Cat, this wild cat has very thick fur and a long tail, which it uses for balance when climbing trees. 26

Margay
The Margay is very similar to another wild cat, the Ocelot. Both cats come from South America, but the Margay is better at climbing trees. 24

Mekong Bobtail
These short-tailed cats came from Thailand, where they often live in temples and are considered a national treasure. 13

Minskin
The miniature Minskin was bred from crossing the Munchkin with the Sphynx. Because of its short legs, it cannot jump as high as some other cats can. 5

Minuet
Also known as the "Napoleon Cat," this breed is a mix of the Persian and the Munchkin. It has thick fur and unusually short legs. 6

Munchkin
The Munchkin is a dwarf cat. It has short legs, but in all other ways is like an ordinary cat. It is named for the "munchkins," who were natives of Munchkin Country in L. Frank Baum's "Oz" books, including *The Wonderful Wizard of Oz* (1900). 5, 19

Maine Coon

Nebelung
This longhaired blue-colored cat has green or yellow eyes. "Nebel" means "fog" or "mist" in German. 6, 18

Norwegian Forest Cat
An ancient breed from Norway, where the cats once lived in forests, these domestic cats are very athletic and love to climb trees. 10, 17

Nebelung

Ocelot
Also known as the "Dwarf Leopard," this cat is found

throughout South America. It has bands and stripes on its back, cheeks, and flanks, and small spots on its head and limbs. 27

Ocicat
An American breed, the Ocicat looks like a wild cat but is a domestic cat. It is a mixture of the Siamese, Abyssinian, and American Shorthair. 7

Ojos Azules
These cats have dark-blue eyes and come from New Mexico in North America. The first one was found among feral cat populations. 4

Oncilla
Also known as the "Northern Tiger Cat," the Oncilla is found mainly in Brazil. It is about the same size as a domestic cat, but less heavy. 24

Oriental Bicolor
Any Oriental-type cat with white on its coat is an Oriental Bicolor. 7

Oriental Shorthair
This breed looks very similar to the Siamese, except that its coat can come in as many as 300 different colors and patterns. 6

Pallas's Cat
About the size of a domestic cat, Pallas's Cat is a wild cat from Central Asia. It has lots of dense fur, and thick, stocky legs. Unlike many cats, it has eyes with round pupils. 27

Pampas Cat
This wild cat, which comes from South America, looks much like a domestic cat. 24

Perfold
The Perfold has a sweet face with large, round eyes. Its ears fold down over its head. 11

Persian (modern)
Once called "Longhairs," Persians are one of the most famous and popular of all cat breeds. 13

Persian (traditional)
This is believed to be the original breed of Persian cat. 14, 16

Peterbald
A rare cat from Russia, the Peterbald is hairless and has a long, slender body. 11

Pixie-bob
The Pixie-bob is a loyal and intelligent breed. It has a short tail and round paws. Rather than the more normal four, some Pixie-bobs have seven toes. 7, 19

Raas
Found on the Island of Raas in Indonesia, this cat is hard to train, and bigger than most domestic cats. 13

Ragamuffin
This large, playful cat has thick fur and a sweet face. It does not reach full size until it is about four years old. 7, 19

Ragdoll
The Ragdoll has beautiful blue eyes. It is one of the largest domesticated cat breeds in the world. 6, 18

Russian Black
Like the Russian White and Russian Tabby, this breed comes from the Russian Blue. 10

Russian Blue
Russian sailors probably brought this beautiful gray cat to England more than a hundred years ago. 10, 17

Russian Tabby
This tabby-colored Russian cat is the same breed as the Russian White and Russian Black. 10

Russian White
Like the Russian Blue, this cat has two layers of short, thick fur. This is known as a "double coat." 10

Rusty-spotted Cat
This is the smallest cat on Earth, and is found in India and Sri Lanka. It weighs around two pounds, which is about half the weight of a domestic cat. 24

Sand Cat

Sam Sawet
This medium-sized breed from Thailand has only recently been discovered. 14

Sand Cat
Sand Cats live in deserts in Africa, the Middle East, and Asia. They can survive without water by using the body fluids from their prey. They hunt by digging, and eat rodents, snakes, reptiles, and birds. 24

Savannah
This wild-looking cat is a cross between a domestic cat and a Serval, a large-eared wild cat found in Africa. Like dogs, Savannahs will follow their owners, and they can be trained to fetch. 5

Scottish Fold
Originally from Scotland, these cats have ears that bend or "fold" down toward the front of the head, giving them an owlish look. 8, 17

Selkirk Rex
The first Selkirk Rex was born in Montana, USA. These large and solidly built cats have distinctive curly hair that feels soft and woolly. 7

Serengeti
Serengetis have an upright posture, large round eyes, and upright ears. They can be shy with strangers. 6

Serrade Petit
This little cat from France has a short coat, medium-sized tail, big ears, and small eyes. 11

Serval
A wild cat from Africa, the Serval is medium-sized and slender. Servals were bred with domestic cats to produce a new breed – the Savannah. 26

Shorthaired Colorpoint
Like the Siamese, this cat loves to "talk." It has dark-blue eyes and a thin body. 4

Siamese
One of the most famous of all cat breeds, these intelligent, lively and very vocal cats have featured in numerous books and films. 13, 17

Siberian
Also known as the "Siberian Forest Cat," this Siberian is the national cat of Russia. 11, 18

Singapura
The smallest breed of domestic cat, the Singapura has large eyes and ears. 12

Snow Leopard
Most Snow Leopards are found in China. They live in high mountains on cliffs and ridges where they can hide easily. 20, 23

Snowshoe
The Snowshoe comes from America and is a mix of a Siamese and an American Shorthair. Snowshoe kittens are born pure white, and they change color as they grow. 7

Sokoke
From Kenya in Africa, this rare breed walks on tiptoes on its hind legs. 15

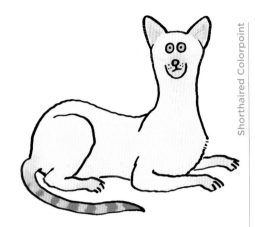

Somali
Somalis are longhaired Abyssinians. With large, pointed ears and a thick, bushy tail, they are also known as "Fox Cats." 15

Sphynx
A very clever breed, the Sphynx looks more like a dog than a cat. Because it doesn't have a coat, it can be a good choice of pet for people who have allergies. 6, 19

Sunda Clouded Leopard
This wild cat has spots on its coat that look like clouds. It can be found on the Indonesian islands of Borneo and Sumatra. 20, 23

Suphalak
A cat from Thailand with a red-brown coat, the Suphalak has bright-yellow eyes. 13

Thai
This old cat breed is related to the Siamese, though it has rounder eyes, and a rounder face and body. 12

Thai Lilac
Similar to the Korat, this cat has silvery-gray fur. 14

Shorthaired Colorpoint

Tiger
The Tiger is the biggest cat in the world. Tigers love to swim, have a powerful roar, and can run at up to 40 miles an hour. 21, 22

Tonkinese
Like the Siamese, the Tonkinese loves to "talk," but it has a much softer voice. It is full of energy and likes to chase, climb, and jump. 7

Toybob
The world's smallest breed of domestic cat comes from Russia. It grows no larger than a regular three- to four-month-old kitten. 10

Toyger
The Toyger was bred to look like a Tiger. It is quite easy to train and can be walked on a lead, and trained to fetch. 7

Turkish Angora
This breed is believed to be one of the earliest longhaired cats. It originally comes from Ankara in Turkey. 12

Turkish Van
Rare cats with blue or amber eyes, or with one eye of each colour, Turkish Vans have white coats with markings only on the head and tail. 14

Ukrainian Levkoy
The Levkoy has a strange appearance, having little or no hair, folded ears, curly whiskers, and almond-shaped eyes. 11

York Chocolate
Named for the US state of New York where it comes from, the York Chocolate has a fluffy, chocolate-brown coat. 6

Sam Sawet

A FIREFLY BOOK

Published by Firefly Books Ltd. 2018
Copyright © 2018 Eight Books Ltd.
Text copyright © 2018 Mark Fletcher
Illustrations copyright © 2018 Jim Medway

First Printing

Publisher Cataloging-in-Publication Data (U.S.)

Library of Congress Control Number: 2018933320

Library and Archives Canada Cataloguing in Publication

Medway, Jim, author
Big cats, little cats : a visual guide to the world's cats / Jim Medway.
Includes index.
ISBN 978-0-228-10107-9 (hardcover)
1. Cat breeds--Pictorial works--Juvenile literature. 2. Felidae--Pictorial works--Juvenile literature. 3. Cats--Pictorial works--Juvenile literature. 4. Cat breeds--Juvenile literature. 5. Felidae--Juvenile literature. 6. Cats--Juvenile literature. I. Title.
QL737.C23M44 2018   j599.75   C2018-900873-3

Published in Canada by
Firefly Books Ltd.
50 Staples Avenue, Unit 1
Richmond Hill, Ontario L4B 0A7

Published in the United States by
Firefly Books (U.S.) Inc.
P.O. Box 1338, Ellicott Station
Buffalo, New York, USA 14205

Printed in China

For Ilia and Enio